LAVENDER M*
by
Michelle Burke

Kiki
and the Flaming
Flamingo

Published by Lavender Health Ltd.

Copyright Michelle Burke 2024

Thank you, as always, to my family for their support in my writing – especially my husband, Paul, and my mum, Mary. Thank you to the Wilson girls, Ros and Zoe, along with our local grassroots football team, who inspired the character of Wilson the Woodpecker. Thank you to Lily and Isla for allowing me to bring them to life. Thank you also to my gorgeous, handsome son Flynn, of whom I am immensely proud every day; currently he has no idea that I have characterised him into a flying fish.

I write with extreme gratitude that you have chosen to read my book. Enjoy the magic of the maze once again …

The Lavender Maze Series
Kiki and the Flaming Flamingo

Author's foreword

It has been nothing but a delight to enjoy the success of my debut book, *Kiki and The Lost Leprechaun,* the first book in the Lavender Maze series. I have spent time visiting schools around the country, reading and delivering character-building workshops. The imagination of a child should always be celebrated and, as I say in my author visits, the moment you open the cover of my book you are instantly, magically transported to the Lavender Maze. This is the beauty of reading.

I very much look forward to writing more instalments of Kiki's adventures in the maze and hope that you enjoy this encounter with Blaze the Flamingo.

A note for adults

As with my previous book in the Lavender Maze series, there is a glossary at the back of this story to encourage your child to extend their vocabulary and learn what those bigger words mean. Words that appear in this glossary have all been emboldened within the story itself.

"Life itself is the most wonderful fairy tale."

Hans Christian Anderson

Monkey Puzzle Tree
Crumbling wall
Iron Gate
Entrance to the Maze
Wilson
Blaze
Clearing

Cravendale Cottage
Nanny's House
Nanny's House
Lavender Pools
Lily and Isla
Flynn
Bridge
Queenie

Chapter 1

Kiki was at school today. It was another one of those incredibly boring Friday afternoons when she was desperate to go home. As she yawned and looked out of the window she realised that she was daydreaming again and thinking about the magical lavender maze that she had found in her garden last December. Ever since her **expedition** to the maze her mind had been **preoccupied** with her adventure. Nanny Stick, as she liked to call grandmother, had always told her stories about how she used to visit the maze when she was a child. Kiki, however, hadn't really believed her until that day in winter when the snow fell hard and icicles hung like crystal swords from the eaves of her house. That was the day she herself followed Nanny Stick's instructions. She had walked up the bridal path to the end of her garden and seen the huge **Monkey Puzzle tree**. She had circled it twice and then discovered the crumbling wall. Nanny's instructions were to place both hands on the wall and shout "LAVENDER!

LAVENDER! LAVENDER!" As soon as she did this the **towering** iron gate appeared and she entered the maze. And oh, what an adventure she had that day. She had met Lucky the Leprechaun who was lost and needed to return to his hometown in Ireland. With the help of the Lavender Maze they had both **navigated** their way to finding him help. What's more, she had helped him jump back into the rainbow that would return him to his home.

The Lavender Maze hadn't been there since, though. Kiki had returned every day after school and skipped along the bridal path, but there had been no Monkey Puzzle tree, no crumbling wall, no iron gate and definitely no lavender maze. It was so disappointing for her.

"Kiki! Are you paying attention?" shrilled her teacher in a high pitched voice. Kiki jumped slightly out of her chair, her thoughts being disturbed by the teacher's **glaring** eyes.

"Yes Miss, I am!"

Kiki glanced at her best friend Ellie who was sitting near the window and smiled. Then she left her daydreams behind until the final hour of school, patiently waiting for her mother to collect her and take her on the long drive home.

Cravendale Cottage was a such a long journey from school and the town. Her house was very remote but **picturesque** and beautiful. She felt very lucky to live in English countryside, surrounded by trees, fields and nature. She also felt blessed that

Nanny Stick lived so close to her. She was in the **annexe** attached to Kiki's house. It was small and perfect for Nanny's needs. It also meant that Kiki could visit Nanny any time she wanted to.

As Kiki arrived back home from school she saw Nanny Stick at her window and gave her a wave. Nanny was making tea and Kiki could see her big hair full of hairspray to add a touch of glamour to her appearance. Nanny always made a big effort, even though she was now eighty-six. She was always neat. And she wore purple lipstick (even though she rarely went out) to match her purple jumper and slippers. She was truly unique and Kiki loved her with all of her heart. No one made toast quite like Nanny Stick. If there was an award for "Best Toast Maker" it would undoubtedly go to her. There was no better **gastronomic** delight than hot toasted bread with butter melting into it.

Nanny Stick moved the vase of colourful spring tulips, opened the annexe window and called out, "Good afternoon Kiki, How was school?"

"Really boring," Kiki replied.

Nanny Stick giggled at her and said, "Take your uniform off, get changed, and then come and see me. I'll get you some toast and we can have a chat." Kiki smiled widely and went through her violet-coloured front door, up the stairs to her bedroom, and got changed. It was early March, still quite cold with long dark evenings. Kiki knew she should wrap up well, and chose to layer a tee-shirt and a jumper with a skirt and tights so she had layers of warmth.

She told her mother she was going next door to see Nanny, opened her front door, stepped through, took four steps to the right and entered Nanny's annexe. She was fortunate that Nanny lived so close to her. Her tummy welcomed the smell of hot toast as soon as she opened the door. Being at school was hungry work so her after-school snacks were an essential addition to her visits to Nanny.

"Nanny," she said, "it's been months since I found the Lavender Maze. Why can't I find it again?" She sat down and began noisily munching her toast. "Don't eat with your mouthful Kiki," instructed

Nanny and immediately carried on, "I don't know why you can't find it again. Exactly the same thing used to happen to me. There is no rhyme nor reason why. I never knew when I would stumble across it. I often went down the bridal path but just could not see the Monkey Puzzle tree. I think the **enchanted** gateway only happens when there is someone who needs your help." Nanny stopped, looked at Kiki, and pushed her glasses higher up her nose.

"Well … I'm going to check again this evening," said Kiki. She finished her toast and picked up her coat. "Put the kettle on Nanny. Let's have tea when I'm back. I won't be long. It's getting dark, and I doubt the gate will open anyway!"

Nanny Stick watched as Kiki eyed up the freshly baked apple cake resting on the side. Then she gave Nanny a **delicate** kiss on her wrinkled cheek and left the annexe, quietly closing the door behind her.

That evening, the **twilight** sky was painted in **hues** of lavender and **indigo**. The sun's last rays were gently fading, signalling the **transition** from day to night. Kiki had a thought that perhaps it was too late to go along the bridal path on her own. But she also thought she wouldn't be very long. And she certainly didn't think she would see the magical Monkey Puzzle tree. So off she proceeded towards the bridal path. It was an even pathway, mainly of mud, and was used by horses in the area so you could clearly see their shoe prints in the mud. It hadn't been raining, so luckily the path was fairly easy to **navigate**.

Whilst Kiki was walking along looking at the strange colours in the sky, she failed to notice what **towered** in front of her. It wasn't until she almost walked into it that she realised it was the Monkey Puzzle tree in all its glory. She stopped herself from gasping – she knew that legend said you must be completely silent in the presence of this tall evergreen tree that almost met the horizon. Its leaves were hard and strong, with sharp and spiky branches that formed what looked like a **symmetrical** puzzle.

For a while Kiki didn't move or speak. She hadn't expected this tonight. She had thought that, by now, she would be bounding back to Nanny's annexe for her cup of tea. But here she was about to enter the **enchanted** gateway of the Lavender Maze again. She was full of **apprehension**. What would she find? Who needed her help? She was afraid. And it was almost dark. But she did know that the maze would guide her and look after her. So she proceeded – doing everything that Nanny Stick had told her to do.

  She circled the Monkey Puzzle tree twice and then she saw the crumbling wall. It looked just the same as last time. **Shimmering** dust floated in the air but she closed her mouth so as not to swallow any and moved closer to the wall. She placed both hands on the wall and in her very loudest voice shouted, "LAVENDER! LAVENDER! LAVENDER!"

Fireworks filled the night sky just as they had before. They were so loud that Kiki put her hands over her ears. Purple smoke was everywhere and she could hardly see. Then, as she moved forwards slightly, she began to see the enormous iron gate grow from the ground in front of her very eyes. She watched as it sprung from undergrowth until it was fully formed. It was a gate for giants, so enormous it took her breath away. She knew as she walked closer what would happen. The gate would creakily open exactly as it happened earlier. She edged closer, walking **cautiously** and slowly, and as she entered through the gate she noticed it was still twilight. It wasn't quite dark yet, but there was no sunlight. The dark clouds were **ominously** low and the Lavender Maze was silent.

Who was she going to find in the clearing of the maze? She knew someone needed her help so she was keen to proceed. She stepped forward with **anticipation** of who she was going to find.

LAVENDER MAZE SERIES

Chapter 2

Kiki walked a few steps towards the clearing of the maze and couldn't believe what was happening. She could see fire. Was the maze on fire? Her casual steps changed to a run. She was running towards the **infernal** dance of flames that glowed through the night sky wondering what this **unpredictable** flickering danger was.

As she reached the clearing she could see huge puffballs of orange and red fire **erupting** around something. She wasn't exactly sure what that something was though. She edged closer feeling the heat on her face from the flames and then she heard a faint moan. It quickly became a loud moan. Someone sounded really upset. The mysterious thing was that the moan was coming from in the middle of the fire.

"Is someone there? Are you in the fire?" Kiki screamed loudly so they could hear her. She couldn't see through the **dense** smoke and was being deafened with the cracking and popping sounds of the flames. She was **inhaling** smoke and the flames were spreading rapidly. She was sure someone was in the fire and she started to panic.

She blinked away some smoke and watched in **awe** as the fire immediately **extinguished**. It was gone as quickly as it seemed to have arrived. There were still **remnants** in the air and ashes were floating around but the fire was completely gone. When the ashes had subsided Kiki saw who had been moaning. In front of her was the most astonishingly pink flamingo. She rubbed her eyes as she wondered if she was actually looking at a real-life flamingo. How was this flamingo in the Lavender Maze surround by fire?

The flamingo stood gracefully on one

slender leg, its vibrant feathers in deep shades of pink and coral. Its long neck was arched in an **elegant** curve and its beak seemed to add to its overall charm. Kiki had never seen a real life flamingo before.

"Are you OK, Flamingo? Did you get caught in the fire?" she asked. "Oh no. You see, I AM the fire," the Flamingo proceeded to explain. "Let me introduce myself. I am Blaze the Flamingo. I live on a Caribbean island called Aruba. It's famous for its stunning white beaches, **turquoise** waters and year-round sunshine. It is such a wonderful place to live. However, I need the help of the Lavender Maze. Are you Kiki? I have heard there is a girl called Kiki here that helps people if they have a problem,"

Blaze continued.

"Yes, hello Blaze. It's nice to meet you, **albeit** under extremely dangerous **circumstances**! But I don't know how I can help you. Usually, the Lavender Maze guides us …" She paused, then asked, "But WHY do you need help?"

Blaze proceeded to tell his story, and what a story it was.

"The day I was born, on the beach in Aruba, a magical **comet** flew over the island. There was a **fusion** of **celestial embers** which meant that the magical comet crashed into another comet in the sky, way above the stars. As they **collided** the ashes fell to the ground and, as I was born, they fell on me! I was **cursed** with magical fire. You see Kiki, every time I flap my wings, huge puffballs of fire **generate**. I become dangerous. No one on the island of Aruba can be my friend because the risk of fire when I am close is just too great. I have lived alone at the end of the beach for many years. My friends visit **occasionally** but they do not stay long for fear that I will start a fire. I have heard that the magical Lavender Maze can help me break the magical comet's **curse** and perhaps one day I can become a normal flamingo again and go back to Aruba to live with my friends and family."

Kiki listened **attentively** to the story that Blaze was telling her and felt **empathy** for him. Imagine not being able to live with your friends and family because you are a danger to them? "Poor Blaze," she thought. "This must be so terrible for him." She was sure the maze would guide them to a way to break the magical comet's curse.

"Blaze," she said aloud, "this sounds terrible! I too am slightly afraid of the flames. But I am here to help you and together we will find a solution. We will get you back to Aruba to live safely with your family and friends and we will break the magical comet's fire curse." She was thoughtful for a moment. "How we do that, though, I really don't know."

"Thank you. I am so very grateful," said Blaze. "This maze is my last hope. I have flown more than five thousand miles to be here. I flew high above the clouds powered by my fire wings. It was such a lonely journey. All the birds avoided me … and I had to be especially careful of aeroplanes! They certainly didn't want a flaming flamingo crashing into them."

"Let's go further into the maze, Blaze," suggested Kiki, "and let's see what we can find to help you. The last time I was here I met a leprechaun called Lucky and the maze guided him back home. So I believe the maze can do this for you too. We just have to trust in the magic." Kiki felt a warm glow inside her. She really did enjoy helping people and was delighted to be back in the Lavender Maze about to **embark** on yet another journey – this time with Blaze the Flamingo.

But before they had even started to

move, they both heard a strange sound. It was a **rhythmic** tap-tap, tap-tap. There it was again: *tap-tap-tap*! And again: *tap-tap-tap*! There was nothing and no one in the clearing except for Kiki and Blaze, so the noise was a complete mystery. Where was it coming from?

Surrounding the clearing were large blooms of giant lavender. It smelt amazing, so calming and fresh. There was a small tree to the left of the clearing, and it sounded like perhaps the noise was coming from there. *Tap. Tap. Tap. Tap . ...* Kiki and Blaze ventured closer to a tiny bird on the top branch. His feathers were **striking** and his beak was **chisel**-shaped – perfect for drilling wood. He also had very strange-looking feet.

"Hello, bird. I wonder if you can help us?" Kiki asked. She could see he was using his beak to **forage** for insects and **larvae** under the **bark** of the trees. On moving closer she could also see that he had a very long tongue with **bristles** at the tip. Kiki remembered from one of her classes at school that this must be a woodpecker. They were **acrobatic** climbers and could move **vertically** up tree trunks because their feet were very strong and their feathers helped them to balance.

"I don't know … *tap-tap-tap*!" replied the woodpecker without stopping what he was doing. "Why do you need help … *tap-tap-tap*?" he questioned as he carried on with his rhythmic drilling at the trunk of the tree.

"My friend Flame," she began, pointing at the flamingo, "needs the help of the Lavender Maze to reverse the curse of the falling magical comet. He wants to be able to flap his wings without puffballs of fire appearing. I am sure somewhere the maze has the answer …?" Kiki's voice trailed off. The woodpecker finally stopped drilling and the loud tap-tap-tapping came to a sudden **halt**.

"Let me introduce myself," he said with an air of **formality**. "I am Wilson the Woodpecker. I have been **resident** in the Lavender Maze for many years, and I am lucky because I can climb trees very quickly and fly right to the top branches where I have a bird's eye view of the whole maze." He paused, then looked straight at Kiki and said seriously, "There is not a corner of this maze that I do not know." He looked very proud as his feathers ruffled slightly under his beak. "I think you need to find the Flower Fairy twins. They are called Lily and Isla. They will be able to advise you which powerful plants in the maze could help you Blaze. They are a **fountain of knowledge**. The Flower Fairy twins know *everything*!" Turning his beak towards Blaze, he said with confidence, "They can help you to find the answer. They don't live very far from here. You will need to follow the maze straight ahead, turn right, turn left, turn left again and then turn right. They have a tiny fairy house just on the corner by the tallest lavender bloom in the maze." Wilson then started to drill again. *Tap, tap, tap, tap*. There was a soothing pattern to the tapping. It very much sounded like music.

"OK, thank you, Wilson. That's very helpful," Kiki **responded**. Blaze and I will set off on a mission to find Lily and Isla, the twin Flower Fairies, and hopefully they can guide us in the right direction to find the answers. We really need the healing properties of the maze to fix Blaze so that he can fly home again to Aruba to live with all of his friends and family without putting them in danger of fire."

Then Kiki turned to Blaze and said, "Are you ready Blaze? Let's go and find the Flower Fairies."

With that, Wilson stopped drilling, wished them good luck and went back to his job. Blaze thought about how strong woodpeckers need to be, and Kiki explained that their brains are very protected. "They need to be," she said, "to stop any injury from all of that tap, tap, tapping!" And off they went, throwing Wilson a wave before heading onwards into the maze.

As they walked, they noticed how **spectacular** the blooms were. They also noticed it was getting slightly cold and evening was fast approaching. The maze wasn't completely dark but it was getting that way and Kiki was aware that they would need to complete their mission quickly because she didn't want to be lost in the dark in the maze.

She repeated Wilson's instructions out loud, "Follow the maze straight ahead, turn right, turn left, turn left again and then turn right." That is exactly what they did. It seemed an awfully long way. Blaze was large and although his legs were very thin and his feet were webbed, they were coping incredibly well with the journey to the fairy house. Kiki, however, was tired. She had been at school all day and it was approaching her bedtime. She was also worried that they would be stuck here in the dark. As soon as those feelings of worry overcame her she **inhaled** through her nose and smelt the lavender **aroma** which immediately gave her a sense of calm. Everything was going to be ok.

LAVENDER MAZE SERIES

Kiki and the Flaming Flamingo

Chapter 3

When they finally took the last turning they saw the enormous lavender bloom on the right hand side and, on walking closer, they stumbled across the Flower Fairy twins' house. It was just as you might imagine a fairy house to look – a tiny white square house with **miniature** windows at the bottom and the top. Lavender hung around the **rustic** front door and a pretty silver bell was screwed to the wall next to the door. Before they could even ring the bell, Kiki and Blaze heard arguing coming from inside the house. They looked at each other wondering if it was Lily and Isla, the Flower Fairy twins. Suddenly the front door flew open and the twins came running out, **oblivious** to Kiki and Blaze who were watching them in **amusement**.

The Flower Fairy twins were not acting as you might think fairy twins should act. No. Lily and Isla were rolling around the ground together shouting at each other.

"That cake was mine! You shouldn't have eaten it!" said one of them.

"No. It was MINE! YOU shouldn't have eaten it!" said the other.

"Yes I should."

"No you shouldn't."

"It's not fair."

"Go away."

"You are the worst sister in the world."

"No, you are."

One of the fairies suddenly looked up and saw Kiki and Blaze. Her eyes opened widely at the sight of Kiki and this striking flamingo.

"Isla … Quick, stand up! We have guests."

Lily helped to pull Isla up off the ground. They both looked completely **bedraggled** and began to straighten their dresses and tidy their hair. "Errrr … sorry

… we were errr … we were just having a slight disagreement. We are Lily and Isla, the Flower Fairy twins." Kiki thought how typical they were of sisters and giggled at them.

"Ooooh, are you Kiki?" questioned Isla. "We knew your Nanny Stick many years ago. We helped her many a time, didn't we Lily?" The twins seemed to have forgotten that a few minutes ago they were scrambling around the ground together and now seemed to be the best of friends. "Yes, we did Isla didn't we. Nanny Stick was amazing. We really miss her. And I'm guessing you are here now, Kiki, because you need our help. Is it for the flamingo?"

Lily and Isla looked at Blaze and Blaze started to tell them his story. "You see, every time I flap my wings like this …" and right then and there he flapped his wings without even thinking. Huge puffballs of fire shot into the evening sky. Lily and Isla shouted "DUCK!" and all three of them, Kiki, included fell to the floor as the fire of blazes wings **smouldered** above them.

Luckily, the fire was higher than their fairy house, so it escaped any damage. But it was quickly **apparent** to the Flower Fairy twins how dangerous Blaze's curse from the magical comet was. Even Blaze was terrified. He hadn't meant to flap his wings. Sometimes it just happened – he had been telling the twins about his curse and his wings had flapped and released the flames.

LAVENDER MAZE SERIES

"Blaze, what a curse, you poor flamingo. I can't imagine being afraid of my own wings," said Isla. Lily agreed with her sister. Both of them had wings – but they were very different from Blaze's. Where Blaze's wings had a very long **wingspan**, pink, fluffy and perfect for flight, the fairies' wings were **intricately** delicate. They were **translucent** and shimmering, and they had been fluttering slightly since Kiki and Blaze had arrived.

The twins were **identical** but were wearing different dresses. Isla's was light blue, ending just above knee with pearl-coloured buttons around the collar. Lily's was light green, also ending just above the knee, but it had gold-coloured buttons around the collar. The twins were beautiful. Both had long blonde locks of curly hair, bright pink lips and, as Kiki couldn't help but notice the most, they had elegant slender fingers.

"We know how we can help," said Lily.

"There is a magical flower in the maze called Fireflower Bloom. It grows way up at the top of the lavender. When it's **harvested** and **crushed** into the **soothing** water of the lavender pools it can **reverse** the magical comet's curse. You would need to drink the **potion**, Blaze, and it will **extinguish** your flames. You will no longer **expel** fire when your wings **expand**. You would be safe to fly home to your family and friends", added Isla.

"There is a problem, though," Lily continued. "We can't reach the Fireflower

Blooms."

Isla butted in, so that she could explain the dangers more fully., "If you fly up there, Blaze, you will be followed by fire, and the fire could kill the blooms. Kiki would not be able to reach the blooms, and we certainly can't."

Blaze, who at first was **elated** at the thought of finding the answer to his problem, now looked **deflated**. He had come all this way to the maze but he wouldn't be able to reach the Fireflower Blooms safely. Kiki too looked disappointed. Surely there had to be an answer. As she was **pondering** what to do, she heard a familiar BUZZZ ... BUZZZZ ... BUZZZZZ. And right there above her, Blaze, Lily and Isla was Queenie, Queen of the Bees, plus ALL of her bees!

"Kiki!" shrilled Queenie in her distinctive **eloquent** voice of authority. "There you are. We have been wondering where you have been." She **swooped** down. "Hello Lily. Hello Isla," she said to the twins with her bee eyes wide open.

"Oh Queenie, maybe YOU could help us," said Kiki. "We need to reach the very top of the blooms to **harvest** some Fireflower, but we can't send Blaze up as it would be too dangerous. As soon as he tries to fly, fire will appear and we can't risk burning the Fireflower because if it's burned then it's useless."

"Oh course. That is not a problem, Kiki. Your wish is my command." And with that she called out, "Bees … come here."

Queenie was the boss and her bees arrived immediately at her command. They swooped down and picked up Kiki. Her feet left the ground and they flew her high into the sky. Higher and higher she went and darker and darker it became. She knew she should feel scared but she didn't. She knew the maze would look after her. The bees flew her north into the sky for what felt like ages. Then they landed her on a branch – not a tree branch, but a branch she had never seen before. "Of course," she realised, "it's a Fireflower Bloom branch."

The tiny **embers** of gold and orange flowers glittered in the dark. The Fireflower Blooms, intricately wound into long stems, gave magical light shows of colour.

The bees were buzzing nearby ready to **swoop** Kiki back to ground level, but first she needed to harvest some of the precious blooms. She reached out her hand to pick a bloom but as soon as her hand touched it she **winced** in pain. The Fireflower was hot, like the temperature of a boiling kettle. She hadn't **anticipated** the heat.

"How very **bizarre**," she said to herself. She had to think **logically**. "What should I do? If it was hot water, I would blow on it to cool it down. Maybe that would work for the Fireflower Bloom, too."

Kiki leant into the bloom and, with her lips closer together, she blew air and oxygen on the Fireflower. The red and orange glow turned blue right before her very eyes. The flower had changed from very hot to completely cold. She quickly picked it and placed it gently in her pocket. Then she repeated her actions several times until there was no more room to carry them. Now she was ready to call back the bees.

Once again, they picked her up and flew her back south. The blooms had been high above the clouds so she had a long way to travel down to the maze. The Fireflowers were safely in her pockets and she would hand them over to the Flower Fairy twins so that they could help Blaze.

Blaze, Queenie, Lily and Isla were all waiting for the bees to return and land Kiki safely back on solid ground.

"Well, did you get them Kiki?"

questioned Lily.

"Yes, look." She removed them, still cold and glowing blue, from her pockets. It was an **aquamarine** blue that was as blue as the sea.

"Here, pop them in this jar," said Isla. "We will keep them safe," she promised.

"All we need to do now," interrupted Lily, "is head to the Lavender **Lagoon**. Just past there are the lavender pools. That's where we can get some water to crush the Fireflowers into."

Now it was Isla's turn to interrupt. "Then Blaze needs to drink the potion and hopefully the curse will be broken."

Blaze was excited but was desperately trying *not* to flap his wings in case he set light to the maze again. "I can't believe this may actually happen," he said looking towards the Flower Fairy twins with huge **gratitude**.

But how far away were the lavender pools? It was really late now and if it got any darker they wouldn't be able to find their way.

Chapter 4

Lily and Isla marched onwards in the maze towards the lagoon. They were still **quarrelling**, this time over who was going to hold the jar of Fireflower Blooms.

"Give it to me, you can't be trusted," Lily said to Isla with a **hushed** voice.

"Absolutely not. You are the clumsy twin,

not I!" replied Isla.

They were bumping shoulders, and Kiki and Blaze were enjoying the entertainment. These tiny **exquisitely** beautiful Flower Fairies looked so **angelic**, yet they had tempers as hot as the fire in Blaze's wings. It was hilarious. Who would have thought these two seemingly quiet fairies were so **contemptuous**.

Kiki and Blaze followed the twins and could hear Queenie buzzing above them. The night sky was now fully developed and the maze began to look very different. It was slightly **eerie** – especially as they could hear the wind howling through the lavender. "How far to the Lavender Lagoon? My feet are so tired," moaned Kiki. She had, after all, been at school that day and hadn't had any dinner. She certainly hadn't anticipated a visit to the maze this evening. She had been sure the gateway wouldn't open and that she wouldn't see the Monkey Puzzle tree. But how wrong she was.

Kiki **refocused** her mind and remembered their **quest** to send Blaze back home. She pulled her chin up, straightened her **posture** and looked ahead. "Let's get on with the mission!" she commanded. With that, through the dark mist she saw the Lavender Lagoon. Its purple waters shimmered and sparkled under the moonlight and she could see lavender floating around the surface. The aroma in the air was very strong and, once again, the calming smell of the maze overcame her. Kiki could feel her shoulders relax and her heart beat slower. She reminded herself that everything was going to be OK. The maze would guide them.

"Over here," called Isla as she skipped around the edge of the lagoon. The lagoon was exceedingly deep. Luckily, the potion required water from the lavender pools, not the lagoon. The pools were all the way round the back of the lagoon and much more **shallow**. Kiki remembered them from her last visit to the maze when she had taught Lucky the Leprechaun to jump in them like puddles! They all moved cautiously around the lake, they knew it was late and didn't want to disturb the mermaids, so they kept fairly quiet. As they completed a **180 degree turn** of the lake they saw the pools ahead. These too had purple water and were the remnants of what had overflown from the lake, creating a **cascade** of pools of shallow water.

"What do you do now?" Blaze interrupted the Flower Fairy twins who were, at that moment, pulling each other's hair! They were, even after all this way, still arguing who should carry the jar of Fireflower Blooms. "If you both don't stop this," hissed Blaze grumpily, "you will drop the jar and smash it. Then I will be in BIG TROUBLE because without those Fireflower Blooms we won't be able to make the potion and I won't be able to go home!!!!!"

Lily and Isla stopped immediately. They both stood tall and straightened out each other's hair, remembering they were not alone and that their **appalling** behaviour had been **witnessed** by others.

"We need Flynn. He will help us," said Lily.

"Who is Flynn?" questioned Kiki.

Lily began her reply. "Flynn the Flying Fish. He usually hangs out in the lavender pools. Sometimes he joins the mermaids in the lagoon …"

Isla interrupted "… but mainly he prefers the shallower waters of the pools …"

Lily regained control of the conversation. "He is fairly small but is the most magnificent colour. He is silver …"

"Not a grey type of silver though," Isla cut in. "Flynn the Fish is SO silver he shines and glistens with a brilliant **lustre**."

"When the sun rays hit his scales," said Lily, talking quickly before Isla interrupted again, "they **refract** the light and create a dazzling display of sparkling reflections that dance across the waters surface casting a **mesmerising** glow in every direction."

Lily, proud of her **poetic** description, took a breath long enough for Isla to jump in again. "Although Flynn is a small fish he **glides** faster than any other through the water and jumps higher than other fish. Not only is he one of the most athletic fish in the water but he has the kindest of hearts too. *Everyone* loves Flynn the Flying Fish. If anyone needs help, Flynn is always there."

The twins took a moment to

congratulate themselves on their beautiful descriptions. And then, just like magic, Flynn appeared with an almighty leap above the pool directly in the front of them. Kiki screamed loudly. She was not expecting such a grand appearance. Her usually steady heartbeat began to race. The stillness of the pool surface **erupted** like a volcano and Flynn sailed through the air, smiling a big fishy grin. He did what looked like a **somersault** in the air and splashed straight back into the water!

"Wow!" gasped Kiki. "I wasn't expecting that!"

Blaze had taken a few steps backwards but his pink feathers had still managed to get wet from the huge splash that tiny Flynn had made. Flynn had disappeared again. Lily and Isla were laughing at the astonishment on Kiki's face. The first time they had seen Flynn somersault out of the water, they too had been taken by surprise. It was unbelievable how such a small fish could create such a splash with his **aerodynamic** moves.

Flynn suddenly **re-emerged** from the water, this time much more gracefully. Kiki looked in awe at his scales that were like silvery shiny coins. It was dark in the maze, but Flynn shone so brightly he lit up almost the entire lavender pool with his **silhouette**. Flynn's smile, too, had drawn Kiki to him. She wasn't sure she had ever seen a fish smile, but Flynn's kind-looking eyes were definitely smiling. She knew that somehow he was going to help them and be part of their adventure.

Isla took the lead and moved towards the edge of the pool. Flynn's head was poking out, still smiling at Kiki and Blaze. Then he turned towards Isla and said, "Hello my favourite Flower Fairy twin. How can I help you?" Kiki could see from Lily's face that Flynn's comment was going to cause yet another argument. She came storming down to the edge of the pool. "Flynn! You told *me* I was your favourite Flower Fairy twin!"

Once again, Lily and Isla looked as though they were going to pull each other to the ground and start rolling around again. But Flynn quickly **intervened**. "Don't be silly girls. You are BOTH my favourite Flower Fairy twins." He flashed his big fishy smile and the twins seemed happy with these words.

"Flynn," Isla said urgently, "we are here to make a magic potion for Blaze the Flamingo. He needs to break the curse of the magical comet, which cursed him at birth …"

"Yes …" Lily continued "every time he flaps his wings, big puffballs of fire appear and he can't live safely with his family and friends. There is a potion that can reverse the curse. We must crush the Fireflower Blooms and mix them with some water from the lavender pools."

"We have the Fireflower Blooms," Isla explain, "but we need some water from the pools.

"OK, my favourite Flower Fairies," Flynn

responded, "I can help. But first, bring over the jar of Fireflower Blooms. Let's lie them on that rock and you can both crush them. Then we'll put them back in the jar and I will add some water from the pools. You'll then need to put the lid on really quickly," said Flynn.

The twins found an edge of the pool that had a flat surface of rock and gently took the lid off the jar of Fireflower Blooms. The deep blue blooms looked alive as Isla and Lily carefully laid them on the rock. Blaze and Kiki watched **curiously**, noticing that Queenie was still observing from above as well. Then the twins stood on the cold blooms with their bare feet. They clasped their hands together and **simultaneously** shouted "ONE-TWO-

THREE", before jumping on the blooms to crush them. It felt like they had been jumping for an eternity when Flynn called out, "That's enough. Quick … into the jar."

Lily and Isla bent down and scooped up the powder-like dust of the blooms, quickly returning them to the jar. And then it was time for Flynn to work his magic. His fish face left the pool surface and disappeared. The moonlight shone on the pool and everything was quiet. Lily and Isla stood by the edge with the lid ready to clamp on the jar, and out of nowhere came Flynn the Flying Fish. He **catapulted** from the water like a rocket heading for space, did three almighty turns in the night sky and dived back into the pool.

The water splashed everywhere as the Flower Fairy twins held out the jar to collect it. "Quickly … close the jar," Kiki instructed. Lily and Isla slammed the lid back onto the jar … and then something quite mystical happened. Flynn's head **emerged** from the pool. Blaze and Kiki stepped closer to Lily and Isla, and they all **huddled** together to watch the jar in front of them in complete wonder. They couldn't believe what they saw!

Chapter 5

The potion looked like it was alive inside the jar. The lavender pool water was no longer a light shade of purple; it was now alight like fire. Orange, yellow and red smoke swirled around the jar as the pool water mixed with the crushed Fireflower embers. Everyone was staring in amazement at the spectacular light show that was being displayed in the jar. Isla's delicate hands clasped the jar tightly as the potion began to mix itself.

They were all interrupted by Blaze whispering, "Do I actually have to drink that?" He looked slightly terrified that the burning colours inside the jar needed to be **ingested** in his flamingo tummy.

"Blaze, we have travelled all of this way and the potion is ready. This is what you have been waiting for," Kiki reminded him. "The Flower Fairy twins' invaluable **ecological** knowledge of the maze plants has enabled us to finally set you free of the magical comet's curse. I knew the maze would be able to help us."

Kiki's voice **echoed** through the maze.

It's darkness provided a huge contrast to the brightness of the jar. The potion lit up the whole area around the pools and, as everyone carried on watching, the light began to dim.

"It's time, Blaze," said Lily.

"The potion is ready for you to drink," Isla added.

"As soon as I take off the lid, you will need to put your beak inside and drink from the jar," Lily instructed Blaze.

"Drink *everything* until there is no liquid left," Isla reminded him.

Blaze stepped forward, careful not to flap his wings. It would be a disaster if he created fire now! He needed to stay in control of his wings and stop them expelling fireballs. As he neared Lily's hand he cautiously lengthened his long flamingo neck and bent it down to the jar she was holding. Everyone watched in anticipation, holding their breath waiting for what would happen next. **Tension** hung heavy in the night air.

Lily slowly removed the lid to reveal the potion that was gurgling and bubbling inside the jar. Blaze lowered his beak into the jar and began to drink. Kiki knew that she wouldn't see Blaze's tongue. She had learned at school that a flamingo's tongue is at the back of its throat. She had also learned that flamingos are born sort of grey but become pink from eating prawns from the ocean. She had loved that lesson. Little did she know then that, just a few weeks later, she would stand in a lavender maze with a real-life flamingo who could talk!

Blaze drank the potion as everyone watched quietly. But when it was gone, nothing seemed to happen. "Flap your wings, Blaze, and let's see if it has worked," said Flynn, whose fishy head was still bobbing around above the water.

As Blaze lifted both of this wings, fireballs appeared. Roaring balls of scorching hot fire shot out in all directions. The potion hadn't worked! Lily and Isla ducked to miss a shooting ball of flame. "Run," screamed Kiki, terrified of what was happening. Fire lit up the night sky once again and was everywhere Kiki turned. She could see nowhere to hide and the flames was edging closer towards her. Smoke was everywhere. It was so thick and dense, she could no longer see Queenie above her or the Flower Fairy twins. She could hear them all, but she needed a visual.

"Jump in the pools … Quick! Quick! Take cover," she heard Flynn the Flying Fish call out. She ran towards the pools. She knew they were only shallow but hopefully the water would protect her. As she fell into the lavender pools she saw that Lily, Isla and Blaze himself had also heard Flynn and taken cover in the pools. As Blaze **immersed** himself in pool water the fire began to extinguish around him and around the maze. They could smell smoke and the ground was sizzling around them. They were all soaking wet, but did not dare move.

They all waited a few moments until the fire was completely gone, and although the maze had fallen silent they could hear Blaze crying. As they sat on the edge of the lavender pool near him, they could see his huge pink tears rolling down his beak.

"I'm so sorry. I am a danger to everyone," he sobbed. "I thought the maze could reverse the magical comet's curse. But it seems I am going to be a fire **hazard** forever. My family and friends will never be safe with me. Kiki, I nearly set light to the whole maze, I am such a danger." Blaze carried on sobbing. He felt so sad.

Lily and Isla sat either side of Blaze looking rather sheepish. "Ummm, eerrrr," they said together, "we forgot to explain that the potion takes one hour to **activate** …"

Blaze's eyes lit up and the tears stopped. "So, do you mean the potion may still work but I should have waited for one hour until I flapped my wings?" he checked.

"Yes, Blaze!" the twins said together again. "The potion may still work but you flapped your wings too quickly. It didn't have time to work its magic."

Isla and Lily looked at Kiki. "Kiki, the potion WILL work. We are sure of it! We just have to wait a bit longer and then ask Blaze to try flapping again."

Kiki didn't know what to think. "What if Blaze tries again in an hour and the potion still doesn't work?" she thought to herself.

"The maze could set light like last time and everyone would be in danger again."

There was nothing they could do but wait until one hour had passed, and then try again. Would the potion work then? Would Blaze set light to the maze again? Only time would tell.

LAVENDER MAZE SERIES

Chapter 6

Kiki was wearing a watch that Nanny Stick had given her last Christmas. It was a digital watch that clearly stated the time. It was 8pm. That was so late. What would her mother be thinking? She had only popped next door to see Nanny Stick briefly after school. She should have

been home for her dinner long ago.
Not only did her watch tell her that but
her tummy did too. She was so hungry.
She was thinking about the homemade
apple cake that Nanny had made with
cinnamon and sugar sprinkled on top of
the crispy pastry.

Blaze had drunk the potion at 7.45pm,
so they had to wait 45 minutes until it
started to work. Kiki was shivering. She
was soaking wet from the pool water
and her face was blackened with smoke
from the fire. She had a burn in the back
of her skirt where a tiny fireball had hit
her. Luckily, she was unhurt but she had
found it extremely scary to watch the fire
emerge from Blaze's wing. Poor Blaze
had been living with this his whole life.

She really hoped with all her heart that the potion would work for him and he would be free of the magical comet's curse.

The maze was cold. There was no sunlight, just the reflection of the moon on the water. They all sat at the edge of the pool in silence, all worried and concerned about Blaze and wishing the next 45 minutes would pass by quickly. Flynn wasn't smiling anymore and Blaze looked bedraggled. His feathers were wet and he was no longer a vibrant pink colour but more of a dull grey colour from the smoke that clinged to his luxurious flamingo coat. Lily and Isla had finally stopped arguing with each other. Everyone was wet, cold and exhausted. They huddled together for warmth and looked at the watch on Kiki's wrist as each minute passed by.

Finally, her watch said 8.45pm and the hour was up. Blaze stood up and said, "What if it hasn't worked? I will be putting you all in danger again. I cannot control the fire if I open my wings and the potion hasn't worked. I will set light to the maze, like last time. You should all go and leave me alone."

"We are NOT leaving you Blaze," Kiki said on behalf of the others. "Friends stick together and we are here for you. No, let's just do this. Are you ready? OPEN THOSE WINGS." Kiki held hands with Lily and Isla and they closed their eyes. Flynn put his head under the water.

Blaze opened his wings.

He opened them as wide as they would span.

Nothing happened.

NOTHING HAPPENED.

They all gasped. No fire! Blaze had opened his wings and for the first time in his entire life they had not produced puffballs of fire. The potion had worked. The Flower Fairy twins had been correct. The crushed Fireflower embers and lavender pool water mixed together had cured Blaze of the curse. He could now return home to Aruba and live happily with his friends and family without being a danger to them.

Blaze lowered his wings but couldn't quite believe he was free of the fireballs. To double check, he opened his wings again. No fire! He closed his wings. To triple check, he opened his wings again. No fire! It had actually worked. The Lavender Maze really did help solve problems. It had been worth the journey here. Blaze had been so fortunate to meet Kiki, Wilson the Woodpecker, Lily and Isla the Flower Fairy twins, Queenie, Queen of the Bees, and Flynn the Flying Fish. Together they had healed him.

"Come here, Kiki," invited Blaze. Kiki ran up to him as he opened his big wide wings safely and pulled her closer, cuddling her and wrapping his wings around her body. Kiki could feel the softness of his pink flamingo feathers. They were comforting and warm against her cold shivering skin. "Thank you,

Kiki. Without you and the maze I would have been a danger forever. Now I can fly home to my friends and family and never set light to anything ever again." Blaze was very grateful.

Kiki knew it was time to let Blaze fly home. Her job here in the maze today was done. She felt sad, as she would miss Blaze, but she knew he had a long happy life ahead of him on a Caribbean beach full of sunshine and prawns! "Now go, Blaze. Fly into the night sky and head home. It's a long journey," she said.

Blaze gracefully extended his long slender legs and with a sudden burst of energy he spread his wings wide, catching the air. He lifted off the floor of the maze pushing his long neck forwards and soared high in the sky. Higher and higher he flew until he disappeared.

Chapter 7

Kiki was still staring at the empty black sky when Blaze had disappeared out of sight. Lily and Isla reminded her that it was really late and she needed to get back home to Cravendale Cottage. It had been an eventful evening. Kiki said farewell to Flynn and thanked him for his help. She knew Flynn was going to be a good friend and she couldn't wait to tell Nanny Stick that she had met him.

Lily and Isla, who knew every corner and turn of the maze, even in the dark, led Kiki back through the blooms. They were turning left and right and left and right and Kiki had absolutely no idea where in the maze she was, but she trusted the twins. Her feet ached and her skin was so cold. She was desperate to go home. But where was the iron gate? Did the twins know? For tiny Flower Fairies, Lily and Isla walked very quickly. They finally arrived at the Fairies' house. "Would you like to come in for some nettle tea and cucumber sandwiches?" asked Isla. Kiki doubted very much that she would like nettle tea and cucumber sandwiches. She wanted Nanny Stick's tea and some apple cake.

"No, thank you," answered Kiki politely. "I really just want to go home but I don't know where to find the iron gate."

Then the magic of the maze did its work. Right behind the Flower Fairy house Kiki saw the gate begin to rise. Its white iron frame was **embellished** with **intricate** swirls and patterns similar to delicate lace. It got bigger and bigger and bigger. The Flower Fairies couldn't even see the top, as their tiny necks could not look up that far.

"Its time for me to leave," Kiki nodded to the Flower Fairies. "Bye Isla. Bye Lily. Thank you for helping us. You have such knowledge of the plants in the maze. I'm so glad Wilson the Woodpecker suggested we find you. You helped us to send Blaze back home. You helped us to break the magical comet's curse. Thank you, Thank you."

The twins smiled at her, thinking that she didn't see Isla step on Lily's toe on purpose. Kiki knew they were about to start tumbling around again. Why did they argue so much? Sisters! She didn't have any **siblings** but if she did she would not be fighting with them. She would be thankful that she had a friend who lived at home that she could always play with. Although she didn't have any siblings, she did have Nanny Stick and they had great fun together. Now she needed to get home. She needed to tell Nanny all about today and she really needed tea and apple cake.

She walked towards the iron gate. This time she was not afraid. She knew the gate would take her back to the crumbling wall and the Monkey Puzzle tree. It opened creakily and as she walked through she looked over her shoulder and waved goodbye to the twins and the darkness of the maze.

LAVENDER MAZE SERIES

Kiki and the Flaming Flamingo

Chapter 8

The time on Kiki's watch said it was 9.30pm. She had never been up this late before. Usually her bedtime was 7.30pm. What on earth was her mother going to say? She would be worried.

Kiki heard the hoot of an owl overhead in a tree as she made her way past the crumbling wall. She quietly passed the Monkey Puzzle tree and began walking along the bridal path. It was difficult to navigate in the darkness so she had to tread slowly, careful not to trip as the path was so uneven. Usually, she would be terrified of the dark but this evening she felt safe. The maze always made her feel safe and secure. She felt like the wildlife of the night was guarding her. The wise owl in the tree was watching her every move.

As she got to the end of the bridal path she could see Cravendale Cottage in the distance with Nanny's annexe next door. The dusty and cobweb-ridden outside lamp was providing much needed light. She wearily **trudged** up the path and could see Nanny waiting anxiously for her at the window. As Kiki got closer to the annexe door, it opened and Nanny Stick ushered her in quickly.

"Kiki, come in, come in. Are you OK? It's so late. Was the gateway to the maze open? I need to hear all about it, but first I have told your mother that you are going to stay at my house tonight. She came around looking for you but I told a small lie and said you were in the bath and that I would make up your bed here …"

Nanny didn't stop to breathe and carried on "… so you can stay here and tell me ALL about what has been happening. Did you find someone to help in the maze? Who needed your help? Did you help them? Who did you meet?"

So many questions.

Kiki answered "I will tell you all about it, but first I need some tea and apple cake."

Nanny sat Kiki on the sofa and helped her take off the soggy wet clothes she had on, with a burn in the side of the skirt. She helped Kiki put on some lovely warm fluffy pyjamas and got a cloth to wipe off the blackened smoke that smeared across her face.

"My darling Kiki, you look like you have been in a fire," said nanny.

"I have nanny, I have. Let me tell you all about it …"

Kiki and the Flaming Flamingo

Glossary

180 degree turn
Turning around half a circle

Acrobatic
Like a circus performer

Activate
To start

Aerodynamic
Forces in the air

Albeit
although, though

Amusement
Something fun and entertaining

Angelic
Like and angel

Annexe
A building near or attached to another building

Anticipated / Anticipation
Waiting for something to happen

Appalling
Terrible, awful

Apparent
Obvious

Apprehension
Cautious and careful

Aquamarine
A shade of blue

Aroma
Smell

Attentively
Listening

Awe
Amazement

Kiki and the Flaming Flamingo

Bedraggled
Looking messy

Bark
Outer layer of a tree trunks and branches

Bizarre
Very strange

Bristles
Short stiff hair

Cascade
Like a small waterfall

Catapulted
To throw or launch

Cautiously
Carefully

Celestial embers
Pieces of glowing fire from space and the stars

Chisel
A tool that carves wood

Circumstances
A chain of events

Comet
A mass of ice or rock in space

Collided
Crashed together

Contemptuous
Expressing disapproval

Crushed
To break into fine pieces

Curiously
Eager to learn

Cursed / Curse
To bring unhappiness and evil

Deflated
Very sad

Delicate
Fine, soft, precious

LAVENDER MAZE SERIES

Dense
Thick and strong

Echoed
To hear it again

Ecological
Living things in the environment

Eerie
Scary, ghostly

Elated
Very happy

Elegant
Excellent quality

Eloquent
Well-spoken

Embark
About to start

Embellished
Covered in extra things to make something look better

Embers
Ashes from fire

Emerged / Emerge
To come out of

Empathy
Understanding

Enchanted
Magical

Erupted / Erupting
Exploded / exploding, like a volcano

Exceedingly
Very

Expand
Make bigger

Expedition
A journey

Expel
Force to leave

Exquisitely
Finely done

Extinguished / Extinguish
To put something out (a fire)

Forage
To dig for and look for

Formality
In a very correct way

Fountain of knowledge
Knows a lot of things

Fusion
A mix / combination

Gastronomic
Very good food

Generate
To make something happen

Glaring
Staring right at something

Glides
Sails through easily

Gratitude
With thanks

Halt
Stop

Harvest / harvested
To cut a crop

Hazard
Danger

Huddled
Close together

Hues
Shades of colour

Hushed
Quiet

Identical
Exactly the same

Immersed
Fully covered

Indigo
A shade of purple

LAVENDER MAZE SERIES

Infernal
Very hot and powerful

Ingested
Swallowed something

Inhaled / inhaling
To breathe in

Intervened
To get in the middle of, to try to sort out

Intricately / Intricate
With lots of detail

Lagoon
A stretch of water near a larger body of water

Larvae
Grubs, worms, caterpillars (for example)

Logically
Thinking carefully

Lustre
A gentle glow

Mesmerising
Can't stop watching

Miniature
Very small

Monkey Puzzle tree
A large evergreen tree

Navigate / Navigated
To make your way through / travel through

Oblivious
Not realising what is going on

Occasionally
Every now and then

Ominously
A sign of misfortune to come

Picturesque
Like a beautiful picture

Poetic
Sounds like a poem

Pondering
Thinking

Posture
They way you stand (tall, slumped)

Potion
A mixture of liquids

Preoccupied
Already doing or thinking about something else

Quarrelling
Arguing

Quest
A long search

Re-emerged
Came out of again

Refocused
Changing your thought

Refract
To make light change direction

Remnants
What is left over

Resident
Living somewhere

Responded
Answered

Reverse
Move backwards

Rhythmic
Like music beats

Rustic
Very old and a bit worn out

Shallow
The opposite of deep

Shimmering
Shining and reflecting

Siblings
Brothers and sisters

LAVENDER MAZE SERIES

Silhouette
The outline of an object against the light

Simultaneously
At the same time, together

Slender
Slim, long, tall

Smouldered
Burned slowly with smoke

Somersault
A tumble in the air

Soothing
To bring comfort

Spectacular
Amazing

Striking
Unusual, something you would notice

Swoop / swooped
To dive or pounce down

Symmetrical
Looking the same both sides

Tension
Stress, emotion

Towering / towered
Large and tall

Transition
Moving from one thing to the next

Translucent
You can see through it

Trudged
Slow walking when very tired

Turquoise
A bright shade of blue

Twilight
Just before dark arrives

Unpredictable
Not sure what is going to happen

Vertically
Upright

Winced
Squeaked or squealed in pain

Wingspan
From the tip of one wing to the tip of the other when a bird's wings are open

Witnessed
Watched something happen

LAVENDER MAZE SERIES

Michelle Burke

Michelle is the author of The Lavender Maze Series. She currently works as a Women's Wellness Coach at Lavender Health Ltd in Rochester, Kent. She lives with her husband, Paul, and three children. She would love to hear your reviews, so if you have enjoyed reading this book, please leave a review on Amazon.

For more information about Michelle and her books, visit: www.lavender-health.com/books

Printed in Great Britain
by Amazon